Akampurira Abraham

Decentralisation, Local Governance and Development

An Aspect of Development

Anchor Academic
Publishing

Abraham, Akampurira: Decentralisation, Local Governance and Development. An
Aspect of Development. Hamburg. Anchor Academic Publishing 2013

Buch-ISBN: 978-3-95489-133-7
PDF-eBook-ISBN: 978-3-95489-633-2
Druck/Herstellung: Anchor Academic Publishing, Hamburg, 2013

Bibliografische Information der Deutschen Nationalbibliothek:
Die Deutsche Nationalbibliothek verzeichnet diese Publikation in der Deutschen
Nationalbibliografie; detaillierte bibliografische Daten sind im Internet über
http://dnb.d-nb.de abrufbar.

© Anchor Academic Publishing, Imprint der Diplomica Verlag GmbH
Hermannstal 119k, 22119 Hamburg
http://www.diplomica-verlag.de, Hamburg 2013
Printed in Germany

Table of Contents

Chapter One

1. Introduction

Communities need a holistic approach to address problems that affect the people at the grass root. Planning from the direct beneficiaries involves decentralization to allow the lower power centers to widely take part in the development of society. Concerns of the grass root people form the need for decentralization and of local governance. People's involvement in planning at various levels from the village level and all local government units makes problem identification and problem solving easier. High participatory levels of all the people especially the marginalized, encourages innovation to source for the appropriate solutions to the common problems that face society. It therefore calls a decentralized system that caters for the voters' preferences while providing for their services. The concerns of the people call for local planning , transfer of power to the public so that services are brought nearer to the people. This research paper will cover the aspects of local government and decentralization such as good governance, democratization, civil society, deconcetration, devolution and delegation and how these link to development of societies.

1.1. Purpose of the Study

The course will aid people and managers to

- Empower the population so that they are able to manage the public affairs themselves.
- Develop skills for good governance and involving the people in making decisions that affect their wellbeing in their respective communities.

Chapter Two

2. Definitions

Decentralization entails the transfer of power, responsibilities and finance from central government to sub-national levels of government at provincial and or local levels (Crow ford, 2008: 7). It is the transfer of the legal, political, administrative and financial affairs and authority to plan, to make decisions and manage public functions and services.

2.1. Deconcetration

This is when the work, duties and responsibilities and associated authority are transferred from the central government to staff located outside the local government units for their performance on behalf of the public. Local government staff may not be given any independent authority to take decision on performance functions at the lower level it directly reports to the relevant ministry at the central level.

2.2. Delegation

Power is given to the local administrative units by the central units to carry out functions on their behalf. It therefore involves transfer of powers to semi independent organizations in the system but accountable to the centre.

In the local government context, delegation means giving power to an individual or body to carry out a function or duty behalf of the public. Procedurally, some duties cannot be delegated. Some of the duties that cannot be delegated in the 1997 local government act include; approval of development plans, contracting loans, approval of annual budgets among others. This is done to avoid errors that are liable to be committed by local authorizes mainly because of lack of enough expertise.

2.3. Devolution

Through devolution, local authorities are given autonomous powers for planning, administration and financial management on behalf of the central government. Devolution involves the transfer of responsibility of performing these roles with legally defined powers. For example Uganda constitutes 111 administrative districts with Kampala as the centre, the federal government of USA constitutes 50 states and one district with Washington D.C as the centre, Denmark constitutes 47 administrative divisions and 98 municipalities. The local authorities have autonomous plans to make and implement development plans in their respective areas.

2.4. Privatization

The private sector is a very important agent in service delivery. Instead of the local government, the private sector is left with a noble responsibility of providing essential services to the population. At times a partnership of the private sector and local governance is suitable in this endeavor for example in extending safe water, energy among other needs of the population.

2.5. Local governance

Shah (2006 : 2), emphasizes that local governance includes objectives of vibrant, living, working and environmentally preserved self governing communities. He stresses its importance in providing a range of local services and preserving liberty to local residents which creates an environment for democratic participation and civil dialogue, and also promoting market led environmentally sustainable local development. It therefore entails citizen – state and citizen – citizen relations which eases delivery of social services to the population. In the era of globalization, these relationships enhance social and economic net works that is meant for sustainable growth and development.

Several theories have been put forward to support the role of local governance in the areas of manageability, accountability, efficiency and autonomy. Some of these theories include the following.

2.5.1. Stigler's menu

Stigler (1957) identifies two principles of jurisdictional design. Its emphasis is on the closeness of the representative government to its people so as to well cater for the citizens. Peoples' right to vote for the kind and amount of services required is another principle emphasized by Stigler. These principles stress the power of the citizens in decision making through the relevant organs. It is also important to have the services closer to the people but in some cases administrative divisions do not adequately cater for the people in terms of service provision. It is also noted that sometimes the power of the people is not exercised since choosing the leaders to represent the local population is not done in a right manner. This is evidenced most especially when the elections to choose leaders are marred with irregularities.

2.5.2. Decentralization theorem

According to the theorem, each public service should be provided by the jurisdiction having control over the minimum geographical area that would internalize benefits and costs of such provision (Oates, 1972: 55) because;

- Concerns of local residents are understood by local governments.
- Fiscal responsibility and efficiency are encouraged if decisions are taken at the local level. Decisions are owned by the real stakeholders and this encourages effectiveness and efficiency in service delivery.
- Layers of the jurisdiction that are not necessary are eliminated.

Concerns of the local people are an underlying cause and effect of local governance. This calls for the people to be involved in planning at various levels from the village level and all local government units. High participatory levels encourage innovation to source for the appropriate solutions to the common problems that face society. It therefore calls a decentralized system that caters for the voters' preferences while providing for their services.

According to Gordon Crawford (2008 : 7), decentralization entails the transfer of power, responsibilities and finance from the central government to sub- national levels of government at provincial and or local levels. This is meant to have the real beneficiaries have power and authority to participate in decision making and implementation of what affects them.

Chapter three

3.Characteristics of good governance

3.1. Rule of Law

Good governance ensures adherence of human rights, a fair and impartial legal framework, freedom of association and fair social justice.

3.2. Participation

An all embracing system where every development partner is involved in the making of decisions. For example a situation where all men and women participate either directly or indirectly in the work plans of both the local councils and at the national and international level. All citizens are given an opportunity of expressing their opinions for proper resource allocation and service delivery.

3.3. Equity and equality

All people regardless of color, sex, age, or tribe should be treated equally for the sake of ensuring the welfare to the population. All members of the society are given equal opportunities and this ensures their good welfare.

3.4. Accountability

This is very important to ensure fairness within the systems. Civil servants, civil society organizations, the politicians and the private sector are accountable to the public. Accountability is in form of resources and the quality and quantity (output) of the work done.

3.5. Transparency

Good communication and free flow of information is the mainstream of transparency. All the information is for all the development partners for proper planning, evaluation and monitoring. This helps to build mutual trust between government institutions, the private sector, civil society and the public.

Consensus orientation. The public policy takes into the account the interests of the population.

3.6. Responsiveness

All the planning is geared towards the needs of all stakeholders. This helps to improve the aspirations of the public and aid government proper planning.

3.7. Strategic vision

For development to take place, there is always a long term goal for leaders and the public to focus on. This is within the historical, cultural and social complexities of a respective community. Once the vision is taken up by the public, they develop a sense of responsibility and ownership.

3.8. Effectiveness and efficiency

The development partners and all stakeholders make sure that processes and institutions make use of the available resources to produce the best output for the entire population. There is maximum service delivery and optimal utilization of the local resources.

3.9. Professionalism

This is meant to upgrade the moral conduct of the government employees to attain the basic minimum code of conduct so as to execute the job of proper service delivery on behalf of the government. The best outcome of the decentralization is economic and managerial empowerment.

3.10. The quest for good governance

This is a campaign that has been going on since 1980's in almost all countries of the world. This is a dream of all partners in development. These include researchers, donors, politicians, intellectuals, management practitioners, and the entire community. All these have realized the need for good governance and democratization in order to arrive at sustainable development. Development will not be realized by mere manipulation of micro and micro economic environment but through proper resource mobilization, allocation and planning through good governance.

The concept good governance has been defined in both political and academic circles for a long time referring to a task of running government. (Hyden 1992). Since 1980's better methods of governance have major dimensions of development theory and practice. The 1989 World Bank Report on the Sub Saharan Africa shows the growing concern of good governance and its impact on economic growth and development.

LeRoy (1992) insists that the following factors must prevail if one is to talk of good governance; Legitimacy of authority, Public responsiveness, Public accountability, Public management effectiveness, Information openness and Public tolerance of other factors in public character.

The global coalition for Africa considers the following elements for good governance.

1. Predictability of the law.
2. Primacy of legality.
3. Responsible government.
4. Constitutional arrangements and human rights.
5. Transparency.
6. Coherence of administrative institutions.
7. Openness and tolerance of the political system.
8. Participation of the people and communication.
9. Favorable climate for the private sector.

Uganda's cabinet of ministers and permanent secretaries during their retreat held in Mbarara on 6th -10th Jan. 1997, whose theme was "The quest for good governance" came out with the following definitions of good governance in Uganda's context

- Good governance is the authority or administrative order which is accountable, transparent, democratic and conforms to the rule of national justice and established norms accepted to society.
- A system of managing society in such a way that resources are responsibly used in a democratic and participatory manner for the maximum realization of human potential and people's aspirations.
- Good governance is a democratically established system of conducting public affair by a society for their own welfare, it is a system that is responsible to the critical needs of promoting human welfare and positive transformation of society. Such system is characterized by adherence to constutionalism, rule of law, accountability, and transparency in the conduct of public affairs.

All these definitions show that good governance encompasses political and leadership systems (both structures and behavior), public sector management, civil society development

7

and efficiency in service delivery. However it should be noted that good governance must not concentrate on mechanic aspect of efficient service delivery. It must focus its attention on qualitative and equity aspects of empowering people.

Chapter Four

4. DECENTRALISATION

Politically, decentralization is a concept that evokes a variety of functionaries such as liberty, self government autonomy and democracy. Alberti, (2011) explains that the global consensus on the urgency of reinventing government is not only manifested in the research efforts that are focusing on how to improve the performance of governance and public administration institutions. He also said that that it also seen in the innovator's readiness to come together to share information and knowledge about their innovations to minimize wastage of resources and time in re-inventing the wheel. Decentralization therefore results into proper resource allocation, proper service delivery, and increased participation of the beneficiaries, transparency and accountability.

Powers to the local authorities are administratively linked to the central powers by the principle of hierarchical subordination. It is technically the process by which some sections, departments of the central government are given corporate body status and considerable independence to carry out certain functions through decentralization process.

4.1. Democratisation.

This is the process of putting in place systems, structures and practices of government to address the following;

- Freedoms (opinion, association, press and worship)
- Periodic free and fair elections of national and local leaders.
- Decent living standards for every member of society.
- Have accountable administrative structures.

Democratization transforms political and administrative institutions as well as behavior to participate effectively in shaping the economic, political and cultural well-being.

In our school system, there is a lot of power centers right from the top down to the students and workers. There is senior management at the top. There are also departments that are manned by heads of departments. At each of these levels, decision making is done to enable proper departmental planning. All the workers at least belong to any of the departments.

With the students body, there is students prefecture of 60 leaders in a school population of 1200 students. Prefects fall into various departments that include; health department, environment, accommodation, academic, discipline and social justice. Students are able to express their views through the school councils and are able to develop skills such as leadership, communication, and respect for others. With this arrangement, there is proper channels and flow of information. This has tended to improve the academic , professional standards of the entire school community.

4.2. Civil Society.

According to Moyo (1996), the concept civil society to be a " free association" or "a self organization" or "a political community".

In this case the civil society is taken as a political community capable of accommodating a variety of individual and associational interests within a pluralist or at least multi centric social frame work in such greater common public good.

Despite the diverse conceptualizations of civil society amongst scholars, there is a consensus that it must be independent of the state. It articulates and defends civil interests; it is not necessarily in basic contradiction to the state. The major interest of the greater part of civil society is not to capture state power but to check its abuse as well as to influence the formulation and implementation of public policy. At the same time civil society is not the same as society. It refers to the political realm specifically the means and process through which citizens shape character of political and economic life in their country.

The pressure and strength of civil society can be verified by the existence and dynamism of organizations such as NGO's, professional and private sector associations and trade unions. To determine the level of decentralization, it is necessary to identify the degree of autonomy and amount of powers, resources and functions that are devolved to local governments to manage their local affairs. Although this is not easy, several indicators of autonomy can be used to give an idea to how decentralization may be assessed. The following questions must be asked;

- Are the political leaders of the local governments elected by central government? Decentralization should guarantee the existence and proper functioning of elected local leadership.
- How much autonomy do the local governments have in the management of the human resource?

- What legal powers do the local authorities have? Can they take important decisions without having to seek permission from the central government? Decentralization should ensure autonomy in decision making at the local government level.

- What is the degree of their financial autonomy? Do they have any specific sources of revenue? Can they borrow or receive grants from the state? Are the sources for local governments constitutionalised or just decided by the central government.

- Does the political system in the country favor decentralization or centralization?

4.3. Good governance, Decentralization, Democratization and Civil society linkages.

Munshi etal, (2009 : 1) emphasizes that governance has gained prominence public debates around the world in recent times because of its importance.

When the paradigms of good governance, decentralization, democratization and civil society are closely analyzed, it becomes evident that they all seek to empower the people to exercise as much influence as possible on their social political and economic destiny. In other words, political, legal, technical and even technological empowerment is the meeting point of good governance, decentralization, civil society and democratization. Anders, (2011) puts it that disconnect between formal and informal institutions that largely explains the problems in capacity building and institutional performance in both the public and private sectors in Africa. Good governance therefore makes it possible for capacity building for economies to grow.

Decentralization is the process that depending on its objectives and the way it is implemented and the prevailing environment, may lead to the installation of the political administrative frame work for good governance. However decentralization is not synonymous with good governance, neither is it the same thing with democratization.

If decentralization does not lead to the empowerment of the people, then it can not constitute good governance. It can also not contribute to democratization or strengthening of the civil society. Decentralization enhances democratic practices and good governance. It serves as a tool of empowering the population at the grass root level with vested responsibilities of allocating resources and discharging outlined duties.

Good governance must be underpinned by a democratic system of government but democracy can not thrive unless space is given to civil society to operate effectively. The efficiency of civil society is enhanced by the process of empowerment that is fostered by decentralization. Empowerment awakens the society's right to monitor and sanction government. Decentraliza-tion especially when it takes the form of devolution, promotes good governance to the extent that it takes the form of devolution promotes good governance to the extent that it creates conditions for the immergence of independent associations and interest groups at all levels of society, it also creates opportunities for a democratic monitoring process.

Decentralization places the decision making centers nearer to the beneficiaries and therefore create opportunities for these beneficiaries to gain access to the decision making elites and thus increase chances for effective accountability and transparency in the conduct of public affairs.

Decentralization and good governance share some imperatives and rationale, good governance is a pre requisite for realization of sustainable and equitable development. Decentralization serves and enhances good governance to the extent that it helps to create a conducive atmosphere for good governance.

Conditions for good governance include high participatory approach and adoption of policies and action programs with an aim of promoting the welfare and security of the people. Implementation and formulation of government policies and the creation of institutional capacity is broad based and encompasses political freedom, maintenance of the rule of law and sustainable growth of society.

4.4. Benefits of Decentralization

It brings services nearer to the people for example women, girls, children and so on since their problems can easily be identified. It is easy to integrate community problems into national policy and service provision to the people.

There is improved spirit among the people to manage their own resources which increases local governance accountability to the people. This therefore promotes a breed of responsible citizens who are able to manage their own resources for sustainable development.

It makes planning, monitoring and evaluation easier at all levels. It therefore increases administrative effectiveness and efficiency. The population is able to identify with what takes place in the day today running affairs of the state.

It creates suitable local development through indigenous means and improved sense of ownership. People can easily identify what is taking place and be able to participate effectively.

It increases local revenue and resource mobilization. This promotes equitable distribution of resources. It minimizes delays in service delivery. This is because bureaucracy in decision making is minimized. It avoids central decision making which is not friendly to the beneficiaries.

United nations (2008 : 16) emphasizes principles of Private- private partnership which include;

- Transparency.
- Fairness
- Accountability.
- Accountability.
- Sustainable development.
- Participation.
- Decency.

In the public- private partnerships the mentioned values help to eliminate corruption and all its forms, promote a high level of environmental responsibility through development of environmentally friendly technologies. They help to human rights, freedom of association, and all sorts of discrimination, abolition of child labor as well as exploitation of labor through payment of low wages and other bad working conditions.

Figure.1 (By researcher on 22/12/2011)   **Figure 2** (new vision photo)

The figure shows the source of water that was constructed by the community with the assistance of funds from local government in Kirigime in Kabale municipality. This water is very essential to the low income earners who can not afford monthly water bills of the piped water by the National Water and Sewage Cooperation. Children are source of labor to fetch water from the wells. This is one of the ways the poor survive alongside the rich in the urban centers. It is however important to note that when there is a problem in pumping water, the rest of the residents in town resort to these particular sources of water. Figure 2 shows students of Butalega primary school who were absent from school. They decided to go to fish as a source of livelihood. This type of phenomena is common in areas that are commercially busy. Children drop out of school and engage in commercial enterprises. The local government need to institute bye-laws to ensure children keep in school. These bye-laws also help to ensure proper environmental management. As evidenced from the photograph, premature fish are caught which can endanger the fish species.

The process of decentralization faces a lot of challenges, for instance power relations at the local government level. There is a tendency of some positions that seem to conflict while workers are executing their duties especially the politicians alongside the technical staff. For example in Uganda local governance, it is not who heads the district whether it is the RDC or L.C.V or the CAO. It is noted that once one of the three is officiating a function the other two will not appear. There is poor attitude that the people have developed against their leaders. They tend to think that they are thieves and because of this problem, politicians have at times decided to usurp powers and responsibilities vested in boards and commissions.

Weak infrastructure and small financial base affects the delivery of services hence poor welfare and standard of living of the people. This is evidenced by the poor state of roads in rural and semi urban areas. Local governments have no enough funds to maintain these roads yet these roads are important for economically transforming these areas.

Figure 3. (By Kate on 23/12/ 2011).   **Figure 4** (by Cornes).

Figure 3 shows one of sections of Kirigime road that is developing a lot potholes and trenches due to poor maintenance. The northern division municipality authorities complain of shortage of funds to maintain the road. Figure 4 shows members of Onekogwok in Gulu district constructing a fence around a borehole. This is a sign of community participation. Otim one of the residents was grateful to Peace Recovery and other development partners to provide the residents with safe water in the area.

Lack of appropriate personnel is a challenge to local governments. The decentralization process needs highly qualified and motivated staff. This is lacking in most areas. At the administrative units staff lacks commitment and motivation.

4.5. State of governance in some selected parts of the world.

It is reported that Africa has nurtured most of the dictators of the millennium. For example, Idi Amin of Uganda, Mobutu of Zaire, Gadaffi of Libya, Mugabe of Zimbabwe and so on. This situation goes with violation of fundamental human rights and general underdevelopment that goes with oppressive regimes. This situation became a concern to the local and international community, such as the International Bank in the 1990's requested political dilapidated countries especially African countries to revise their styles of governance. It was noted with concern that most of these countries had resorted to one party system and abandoned the multi-party type of democracy. The international community set the pre- conditions for international aid basically on good governance principles. Despite all this effort, there was little trust in governments' transparency and efficiency which resulted still into shaky democracy.

The initial enthusiasm with the global resurgence of democracy may have been too euphoric and somewhat naïve. Stagnant transitions, the increasing fragility of democratization processes as well as the realization of incomplete or imperfect nature of the new democracies have watered down initial expectations. In many parts of the world democracy is fading, eroding or falling, disillusionment about democracy has replaced the optimism that marked the early 1990s as elected governments are riddled with corruption, incompetence and instability. (Santiso 2002, 157)

Governance in such countries has thus remained in a state of chaos despite the intervention by the international community. To confirm Santo's ideas the following incidents are clear testimonies;

- Human rights abuses after 2005 Ethiopia national elections.
- Outright violence in Kenya after the rigging of the 2007 elections.
- State inspired violence by Zimbabwe government after the March 2008 national presidential elections.

Sanitos has added that while the new democracies possess all the formal institutions of democracy, these often remain empty shells, failing to function effectively and to provide the necessary checks and balances. The Kenya Electoral Commission (KEC) and ZEC could be cited as examples of such empty shells. Other unfair practices noted was reversal of official political term limits in countries like Malawi, Nigeria, Uganda, Cameroon, and Zambia. All this is done to keep in power for the sake of siphoning national resources for their own families an infringement to good governance.

NEPAD has adopted the definition of good governance provided by Kofi Annan to mean the means of creating well-functioning and accountable political, judicial and administrative institutions, which citizens regard as legitimate and in which they participate in decisions that affect their daily lives and by which they are empowered.

This institution aims at providing an atmosphere of transparency, promoting democracy and human rights, ensuring accountability and participatory governance. It is noted with concern that development cannot take place without true democracy, good governance, respect for human rights and preservation of peace. Global standards of democracy include pluralism where the people are allowed to choose their leaders from their respective parties periodically. NEPAD has done a lot to towards democracy and good governance. Political Government Initiative has been encouraged to restore principles of rule of law, democracy, transparency, and respect for human rights, integrity and love for one another. In addition commitment to good governance, human rights and democracy is made to the declaration to the on Political, Economic and Corporate governance and Democracy. This Declaration commits the heads of state to achieve the following:

- The equality for all before the law.
- Freedom of association that includes the right to form and join trade unions, political parties without deviating from the supreme constitution of the land.
- Ensuring that there is equality of all citizens   regardless of the color, sex, tribe or ethnic group as enshrined in the constitution.
- Adherence to the separation of powers where every arm of the government independently does its role.
- The citizens' inalienable rights to choose their leaders through a system that is well spelt in the constitution. This should be done periodically after the fixed term of office expires.

All measures to have good governance are enshrined in the declaration. This is meant to provide a political environment so that all citizens participate in the political process. This also provides for the accountable governance, adopting clear codes, indicators and standards. The people will have a will of participating in the affairs of the nation and this result in the sense of owning systems and love for the respective nations one of the biggest challenges in many countries with no good governance is that people in these communities do not have a real feeling for the state. The end result has always been lack of self confidence, high crime rate, and poor political will. High rates of corruption have rooted our societies and this creates lack good governance and proper accountability. This has increased the suffering of the people especially the marginalized.

4.6. Relationship between democracy and development.

Local governance and decentralization breeds to democracy which entails the following;

- Decentralization of powers from higher to lower levels and this leads to proper planning and policy implementation. Policy will be relevant to realities of community needs.
- People's participation in policy making, decision making leading to development.
- Gender equity where there is increased involvement in politics and other decision making organs.
- Creating an enabling political environment that will encourage both indigenous and external investors. This will in turn result into economic progress.
- Civic education that helps the people to elect potential leaders.
- Improve empowerment in form of both skills and capital which helps people to develop their economic status, education status and standard of living.
- Freedom of speech, association, which creates innovativeness in economic activity involvement. This increases on economic activity and trade a sure deal to improve on the balance of trade.

4.7. Decentralization . A policy for social service delivery and rural development in Uganda.

Decentralization involves the transfer of administrative powers from the central to regional or local governance. It is basically done to ensure essential good governance and participation in discussion making, mobilization of support for development, accountability and planning.

Decentralization can also mean system in which power is planted to local authorities or a process in which governance is moved from the centre to a decentralized system. Ichimura etal (2009 : 1) emphasizes the trends in the actions of decentralizing the budgets with appropriate interventions so as to strengthen the financial position and financial autonomy of local power centres. Decentralization programs became more pronounced in 1950's and 1990's and in Africa they followed the recommendation of World Bank to local and autono- mous level. The reason was mainly to ensure good services delivery like health, education, water and sanitation to local level while the government was taking.

Decentralization there fore aims at addressing peoples needs at grass roots because it is a recent, development still on efficiency economic effectiveness, performance and accounta- bility.

Under decentralization, power is taken away from the state or central government and is given to local government in terms of logical, political administrative and financial authority to plan makes decision and manage public function and allocation of resources so as to ensure that the benefits reach the targeted population in deeper areas. Widmalm, S. (2008 :25), empha- sizes that the idea of a federal structure where power moves from the centre to the districts and states which includes political and administrative power. How much power should be decentralized and which tasks to move from the centre to the peripheral areas would deter- mine the success or failure of the decentralization process.

On the other hand rural development generally refers to the policy of improving the quality of life and economic well being of people living in relatively disadvantaged densely and sparsely populated rural areas. It has a motive promoting the welfare of people in rural areas through eradication of poverty, disease hunger and illiteracy.

Decentralization continues to be the corner stone of government's efforts to improve systems governance to faster economic growth. The process is seen as a means of promoting devel- opment in general. Improvement of service delivery on the ground government has decentral- ized the delivery of health, education water and agricultural extensive services to local governance and this is done to improve the capacities of local governments for effective planning management and implantation or related policies.

Decentralization has emphasized prosperity for all: this is a program which aims at tackling poverty at have household level. Its main focus is on commercialization of agric, enhancing food security and nutrition and promoting value addition and product stability. The government has assisted households in zoning and enterprise selection based on current and predicted future demands and price at both regional national and international markets.

Decentralization has helped on assisting households to form business groups' cooperatives so that they can produce big in big quantities and this has helped to boost the export sector. It has emphasized the formation of Area cooperative enterprises (ACE) in rural areas. The government has introduced a new initiative trying to revive the trend of poverty. Cooperative at local level based on lessons learnt from the failure of earlier cooperatives. These programs are implemented for effective coordination and this provides a very conducive frame work with in the people very conducive frame work with in the people in rural areas e.g. the restructuring of the NAADS program was promoted by wide spread out cry over its lack of performance and this has laid a good basis for the eradication of poverty in rural areas.

Decentralization policy has also enabled people in rural areas to access financial credit though community mobilization and formation of SACCOs (Savings and Cooperative Organizations). This helps in ensuring efficiency and effectiveness and resource allocation, increased productivity linked to marketing systems at both local and national levels.

 Decentralization has also led easy implementation of poverty eradication programs such as introduction of the National Agricultural Advisory services (NAADS) ; a program for modernizing agriculture in rural areas. It is intended to ensure that farmers increase their farm productivity and profitability so as to learn better incomes hence development.

Through decentralization the government has introduced non sectoral conditional Grant (NSCG). This assist local government in empowering rural communities to implement community projects in order to increase their incomes. It seeks to promote community participation empowerment. Ownership and team work in the process of service delivery.

Decentralization has also ensured participatory development of village maps in places where there are resources. This makes the community aware of the potential wealth around them. This helps them in discovering their wealth hence helps in the process or service delivery for example oil discovery in the Albertine region in North Eastern Uganda.

Decentralization has empowered village development committees in rural areas to implement non sectoral conditional grant projects and therefore it is possible for parishes to collaborate on infrastructure development projects which are too large to be handled individually such as repair of a common road/ feeder road. This program provides a solid ground on which to mobilize people in rural areas. However corruption has been a major challenge while delivering services to the people for example, according to the audit report (2013), shoddy work was done on several roads in Kabale and more than Ush. 52 million was found an accounted for in Kabale, Hamurwa, and Katuna Town Councils. (New Vision 21st Feb 2013).

Calder, A (2008 : 1) emphasizes that effective corporate is transparent, protects the rights of shareholders, includes both strategic and operational risk management for handsome earnings and holds the directors accountable for of business, and ensures that directors exercise their fiduciary duties responsibly. In Uganda decentralization has led to the development of the sector strategic investment plan (SDIP) sense 2003 the ministry of gender labor and social development has been spear leading implementation of the social Development sector strategic investment plan in rural areas.

Decentralization has also led to the development of the sector strategic investment plan (SDIP), Since 2003 the ministry of gender labor and social development has been spear leading implementation of the social; development sector strategic investment plan in rural areas. This aims at interacting progress with economic growth and sustainable development.

Decentralization has led to better education in rural areas. This deals with UPE and USE, Primary enrolment ratio in Uganda jumped from 67% in 1995 to 79% in 2000, and 90% in 2004. However access to education by the people in rural areas has increased at a lower rate than in the rest of the society. This has kicked illiteracy in children both boys and girls, schools have been build in rural areas to promote education and this has brought development in rural areas.

Decentralization has emphasized the need of the people to have good health. Every sub county in Uganda and parish has a health centre or clinic that is supported by the government. These local level institutions have been entrusted with resources to finance primary health care centers, district hospitals and referral hospitals. This helps in the reduction of child mortality rates and maternal health which is a result of decentralization hence rural development. Due to the fact that every sub county in Uganda and parish levels at large must have a health centre on its own powers supported to the government has been another social priority in Uganda and local level institutions have been entrusted with resources to finance Primary health care enters, district, hospitals and referral hospitals. Outcomes in the health sector are ambiguous for example delivery to health services are being successful and report an increase in access to health centre over a time for example there has been the reduction of child mortality rates and maternal health which has all been due to decentralization which has brought social economic services delivery that has led to rural development. There is however a big concern of lack of drugs and medical personnel in these health centres. Uganda's doctor–patient ratio is 1: 15,000 compared which is far below the recommended World Health Organization ratio of 1 : 10,000. This type of situation tantamounts to poor health of the population in the rural areas despite government heavy funding of the medical sector.

Decentralization has led to people in rural areas have access to safe water for domestic use. Rural water coverage jumped from 55% to 60% between 2003 and 2004. This shows that there has been significant improvement in water provision particularly in poor areas. This has reduced water born diseases like typhoid, malaria hence promoting good health and increasing the life expectancy of people in rural areas. However, there is a lot to address in the sanitation sector. According to WaterAid report Uganda is still lagging behind in terms of better sanitation to the population, by only 34% compared to the required 72% set by 2015.(Daily Monitor, 21st Feb 2013.

Decentralization has promoted gender equality in rural areas at every level of leadership women are given a 1/3 of participation in terms of decision making, though 80% of women employ themselves in agriculture they decide what to do with their products. At every level of leadership beginning with the local councils both women and men engage themselves in co-operative organizations like the integrated rural development programs where women are given powers of leadership.

This is done to facilitate women with families with loans to raise goats, pigs cows and hens and this has led to development with in the community.

Decentralization has led to participation of all people in development of rural areas. Powers to decide matters closely affecting people at local level have been given to the local councils all people have been able to participate in the making of decisions about matters that affect them. They can be mobilized at the local level in relation to a wide range of issues. Local councils can act as an interface between the state and the society. This has led to democracy hence better service delivery in rural areas. Choi, J. etal (2008 : 132) explains that to obtain sufficient control to regulate the complexity of corporate activities, stakeholders need to be introduced as co- regulators. This will minimize shifting blame, corruption tendencies and increasing community identity to their programs.

Decentralization has led to infrastructure development. Decentralization has responsibility to finance infrastructure development at local level e.g. construction of community roads, hospitals, tapped water in the rural areas. This has helped the transport and communication of goods from inaccessible rural areas to market centres. This has resulted into creation of other markets to meet the demands of people hence better service delivery in rural areas.

For social economic service delivery to be attained in rural areas, the government should set broad goals of changing the dominant state controls through decentralization. This lays some impacts in strengthening civil society hence development in rural areas. Another area to tackle by the government is corruption which has reached unbearable levels. Hon. Kadaga (2013) stressed that corruption has attacked institutions, Parliament inclusive. As a speaker of parliament she noted that sign attendance book for the sake of earning allowances but do not attend the sessions, a situation that has led to loss of public funds. (Daily Monitor, 21st Feb 2013).

Decentralization policy is one of a number of national resistance movement (NRM) policies implemented as part of political strategy instead to bring about fundamental change in state society. That strategy is based on the national Resistance Movement (NRM) analysis of the basis forces at work in Uganda and in particular of the source of the earlier destructive past independence conflict.

Decentralization in its myriad forms has been the subject of much interest in Africa in the 1996's, a reaction against the general failure of attempt from 1960's onwards to promote development through strong and centralized bureaucratic state. Democratic sub- national government is seen as a major contributor to the emergence of a strong civil society. The standing point of the strategy was the incorporation of as many groups as possible in a government of National Unity to operate for a strictly limited interims period.

Primary education is partly a success story in Uganda, primary school enrolment boomed with the introduction of the government's ambitious universal primary education (UPE) program in 1997. The net enrolment ratio jumped from 67 percent in 1995 to 79 percent in 2000, reaching 90% in 2004. Moreover, access to education by the poor has increased at a faster rate than in the rest of society. This is indicative of the success of the universal primary education in Uganda which has licked illiteracy in children both boys and girls which has been due to decentralization policy, that every society must have a school nearby to promote education which he brought social economic delivery for rural development. However, there ia a lot of public outcry on the quality of education being offered. For example Francis, K (2013), stresses that, lack of enough teachers where in some instances one teacher handles 80 children cripples the quality of education in primary. Another concern noted is teachers and pupils absenteeism. All these affect student learning and this has continuously yielded poor results especially in rural areas.

At every level of leadership beginning with the local council one due to decentralization as economic development is concern, both women and men engage themselves in co-operative organization for example the on governmental organization like integrated rural development programs where women are given powers of leadership and in National Agricultural advisory services (NAADS) to facilitate women with their families with loans, animals like goats, pigs, cows and high breed hens to look after which has led to development with in the community and it is through decentralization policy that has brought social economic service delivery for rural development and all these have been brought about by the government at all levels of leadership for example district to local council one level.

There has been a remarkable degree of democratization in Uganda through local council elections. And farmers have to decide matters closely effecting them at the local level. They are have been given powers to able to participate in the making of decision about matters that affect them. They can be mobilized at the local level in relation to a wide range of issues. The various local councils can act as an interface between states and society which means in leadership selection in terms of voting everybody has authority to participate and choose the person who is ready for development since democracy is available as it is the government of the people for the people and by the people which all is done through decentralized policy that brings all these social economic programs meant for development.

Infrastructural development is one of the sectors that has been addressed through the decen- tralization policy. The local government have responsibility to finance infrastructural development for example local construction in the district both at the head equators and rural areas and as decentralization is concerned Agriculturalists there achieve a great chance of easy transportation of agricultural products for example sorghum, tomatoes, potatoes, Matooke, rice, beans and many others. This increases market accessibility and therefore a need to construct roads in order to favor transport activities and participation for both people for development in such a way.

It is through decentralization policy that brings all these social economic services delivery for development.

Chapter Five

5. Recommendations

Local government institutions both in rural and urban settings should develop strategies for capacity building in terms of training the workers and raising funds to provide services to the people. These funds are meant to provide safe water, upgrade roads, build schools and providing health care services among other needs of the community. Special program for capacity building for women should be built at both the central and local government.

It requires a comprehensive and holistic training expertise and resources to catch up with the global information technology to overcome global challenges such as environmental management, rural development, disaster management and many others that affect economic growth and development across countries.

Project evaluation and implementation especially at local levels should be emphasized to overcome challenges of corruption and misappropriation of public funds. Also proper procurement and property disposal procedures of public assets should be put in place for proper accountability if public funds.

To ensure equitable distribution of resources between rural and urban areas, there is need for proper planning and commitment of all partners such as the community, civil society, public sector and private sector.

There is need to invest in academic research which helps to build long term institutional capacity for the good of the people of a particular locality. Research also identifies areas of most need where government should invest more resources for the maximum public benefit.

Whereas a report shows improvement of improved governance in Uganda in respect to defending the constitution and supremacy of law, a lot needs to be desired. Many issues regarding governance still need for political reforms. There is still need to restore democracy and fundamental human rights. The government of Uganda should get committed to restoring democracy and the rule of law.

Deliberate policies to cater and care for the elderly should be emphasized in all courtiers'. In Uganda, there is no policy to ensure the proper welfare in the old age. One works hard at the young age and contributes tremendously at this stage and ends badly when he no longer has strength to work. Retiring age in this country is 60 years for the public servants and there is no work given to these people yet they are somehow have some expertise and productive.

Promotion of human rights should be emphasized in all countries. In some societies human rights are violated especially under the context of political horizons. Human rights institutions and civil society organizations should be left to do their work. This includes freedom of expression and reducing poverty in many societies. I have heard talk of areas claiming to peaceful because of the absence of war but when the rate of suffering is escalating because of poverty. I have seen very little freedom with the people who are poor. They cannot afford descent dressing, food education, accommodation and this poses a threat to fundamental rights of a human being.

Multi-stakeholder involvement in better practices to increase transparency and accountability should be emphasized. A lot local involvement is needed to protect the natural resources. Through decentralization countries have embarked on forest management for a sustainable resource management. Greater institutional capacity at the national, regional and international level needs relevant local policies for both human welfare and natural resource management.

Several workshops should be organized to share ideas and experiences on decentralization and local governance and this will help to improve the existing governance. This could widen the balance of power among different government levels and improve people's participation in government affairs such as service provision like water supply, health, forest management and choosing leaders through regular elections.

Important aspects of e- Governance should be adopted in all countries on the globe. These include improved infrastructure, improved computerized systems, standardization, capacity of using   local language in computer systems, ability to change the mindset of the population and government staff on knowledge net working for improved and better governance. e. Governance system is good for organizational development that is intended to delivery of social services, accountability and effectiveness. Piaggesi, (2011: 4), explains that e- Governance is the use of information technology to the processes of government functions and duties to bring about Simple, Moral, Accountable, Responsible, and Transparent (SMART) Governance. It makes government processes open to citizens which ensures government accountability that ensures transparency and effectiveness.

In Uganda introduction of e–Government systems are just taking root. There new administrative methods employed such as EFT, e- tax systems and compulsory training in secondary schools in the next two years to come. This however is meeting a lot of challenges such as lack of appropriate infrastructure, computers, and un reliable energy sources. There is no electric power in most parts of the country especially rural areas.

Chapter Six

6. Conclusion

Good governance is responsible for poverty reduction as evidenced from the workshops of the World Bank and Development Assistance Committee. In its attacking poverty report, the World Bank (2001: 15-19) defines poverty as a multiple human deprivation as well as social and political dimensions. This needs society empowerment to participate in designing policy to increase household incomes, access basic services and freely participate in political processes. Many governments have adopted decentralization and local governance as a way to improve service delivery to the people. However this good practice has been hampered by lack of accountability, lack of adequate financial resources and poor democratic practices. Local governments need to integrate both economic and institutional reforms in countries especially hit by poverty in order to realize economic growth and development.

It is important for countries to promote decentralization that helps in devolution of powers to local government. This helps the local authorities the power to cater for the needs of the people such as employment, trade and business, shelter, socio- economic infrastructure, recreation and transportation. All measures of good governance are necessary to provide a political environment that allows all citizens to participate in the political processes in their respective nations. This includes having clear codes, indicators and standards of participating in the affairs of the nation. It will result into citizens owning the systems and developing a feeling for the state.

Acronyms.

CAO- CHIEF ADMINISTRATIVE OFFICER.

CBO- COMMUNITY BASED ORGANISATION.

DAC- DEVELOPMENT ASSISTANCE COMMITTEE.

EFT- ELECTRONIC FUND TRANSFER.

KEC- KENYA ELECTORAL COMMISSION.

L.C.V.- LOCAL COUCIL FIVE.

NGO- NON GOVERNMENTAL ORGANISATION.

NEPAD- NEW PARTNERSHIP FOR AFRICAN DEVELOPMENT.

UNDP- UNITED NATIONS DEVELOPMENT PROGRAM.

ZEC- ZAMBIA ELECTORAL COMMISSION.

References.

Alberti, A. (2011). Good Practices and Innovations in Public Governance : United Nations Public Service Awards Winners, 2003- 2011.

Anders, G.(2010). In the shadow of Good Governance : An Ethnography of Civil Sevice Reform in Africa. Afrika – Studiecentrum series, V.16. BRILL Inv.

Colfer, Carol. (2005). Politics of Decentralization : Forests People and Power. New York : Earth scan.

Choi, J. (2008). Institutional Approach to Global Corporate Governance : Business systems and Beyond. International finance review ; Volume 9 emerald.

Christopher Mbazira, (2008). An Assessment of the Findings of Uganda's Country Self-Assessment Report under the African Peer Review Mechanism. Human Rights & Peace. *Democracy and Good Governance:.*HURIPEC Working Paper No. 19

Crawford, Gordon. (2008). Decentralization in Africa : A pathway out of Poverty and Conflict? New York, London: Amsterdam University Press.

Daily Monitor (21st Feb 2013).

Fallete, Tulia. (2010). Decentralization and sub national politics in Latin America. London, New York : Cambridge e Text.

Francis, K. (2013). Districts need more teachers recruited.(New Vision 21st 2013). Kampala.

Hoger Bernt, Developing Uganda page 159 fountain publishers Kampala.

Ichimura e tal (2009). Decentralization Policies in Asian Development. Singapore : World Scientific Co. Pte. Ltd.

Koffi Annan, (2008). Partnerships for a global community (1998).

Geotz. A. M (1998).Impacts of decentralization on health behaviours in Uganda,

Mossialos, Elias. (2010). Health systems Governance in Europe Law and Policy. London : Cambridge University Press.

Munshi etal, (2009). The Intelligent Person's Guide to Good Governance. India : Sage Publications.

Nelson,Fred. (2010). Community Rights, Conservation and Contested Land: The Politics of Natural Resource Governance in Africa. New York: Earth scan Ltd.

New Vision (21st Feb 2013). Kampala.

Piaggesi, Danilo. (2011). Global strategy and Practice E-governance : Examples from around the world. New York: Information science reference.

Querejeta, Marie Joes. (2008). Net works, Governance and Economic Development: bridging Disciplinary Frontiers. New York: Edward Elgar Publishing, Inc.

Shah,Anwar. (2006). Local Governance in Industrial countries. Washington: Library congress Cataloging.

United Nations (2008). Guidebook in Promoting Good Governance in Public- private Partner-ships.

Widmalm, S. (2008). Decentralization in Africa. A pathway Out of Poverty and Conflict. India : Sage Publications.

Okiidi J.A and Guloba. M (2008), Decentralization and development; Emerging issues from Uganda Experience " Berlin international workshop".

Decentralization in Africa: A stocking survey African religion working papers by Ndegwa S, N 2002, Paper series

Decentralization in Uganda "Hand out" **Bibliography**

Uganda poverty status report, (2001) (Milestones In The Quest For Poverty eradication) Ministry of finance planning and Economic development, Kampala.

http//www.encyclopedia.com.